AMERICAN LANGUAGE REPRINTS

VOL. 4

A
VOCABULARY
OF
POWHATAN

compiled by
Captain John Smith

With two word-lists of
Pamunkey and Nansemond
from other sources.

STUDIARE · APPLICARE · CREARE

Evolution Publishing
Merchantville, New Jersey

Reprinted from:

John Smith. 1624. *The Generall Historie of Virginia, New-England, and the Summer Isles with the names of the Adventurers, Planters, and Governours from their first beginning An. 1584 to this present 1624.* London.

with additional material from:

Edwin A. Dalrymple. 1858. *Historical Magazine and Notes and Queries Concerning the Antiquities, History, and Biography of America.* 1st ser., Vol. 2 p. 182.

and

James Mooney. 1907. "The Powhatan Confederacy." *American Anthropologist.* Vol. 9, p. 146.

ISBN 978-1-935228-22-6

CONTENTS

Preface to the 1997 Edition

The Powhatan Indians, a confederation of tribes known by the most commonly used name of their paramount chief, were the inhabitants of that part of Virginia first settled by the English colonists in 1607. Captain John Smith, widely known for his rescue by Powhatan's daughter Pocahontas, was one of the original colonists. He published several books on his travels (the 1986 edition of his works edited by Philip Barbour is the definitive edition); a brief vocabulary of the language with a few example sentences was given in the *Map of Virginia* (1612) and reprinted in the *Generall Historie* (1624). The *Generall Historie* includes much of his earlier publications as well as material that had not been published before.

The original manuscript sources for this vocabulary, like those for most of Smith's works, are not known to survive; the works are known from their published forms. Some modern scholars believe that Thomas Hariot, a scholar who went to what is now North Carolina as part of the expedition known as the Lost Colony, prepared a vocabulary of the language used there, a language related to Powhatan. There is no firm evidence to support this, but several Algonquian words were included in Hariot's report, published by Richard Hakluyt in 1588 and almost certainly available to Smith. Smith's relative ease in communicating with the Powhatans suggests some preparation in an Algonquian language, but this facility could also derive from the experiences of his life, which had demanded great adaptability (Barbour's 1964 biography remains the best source on Smith's life). It is also conceivable that individual Powhatans could have learned some English prior to 1607, through contact with earlier explorers, fishermen, or survivors of the Lost Colony, but again there is no evidence for such knowledge. Much like Smith, however, their prior experiences with culturally and linguistically different groups (including the Spanish, four decades earlier) would have encouraged flexibility in the development of communcation skills, and in all likelihood Powhatans learned English more readily and quickly than the colonists learned Powhatan.

The Powhatan language was formerly classified with the Central Algonquian group of languages (e.g., Michelson 1933, Bloomfield 1946), a group that includes such well-known languages as Cree, Ojibwe, and Shawnee, but that classification has since been revised. Powhatan is now classified as an Eastern Algonquian language, a category that includes the physical and cultural neighbors of the Powhatans – the Delawares (or Lenni Lenape, speakers of Unami and Munsee) and Nanticokes – and the division between the eastern and central groups is thought to have considerable time-depth (Goddard 1978a, 1978b:586-87). There were several variant dialects of Powhatan (Gerard 1904; Siebert 1975:287-88, 195-96), but recorded information permits little more than their identification.

In working with the Smith vocabulary we are confronted with problems of orthography typical for the period. Vowels in period handwriting are often easily mistaken, even in the hands of professional copyists, and several consonants can also be confused. This is true not just for modern readers, but also for their contemporaries; comparison of multiple copies of the same document will reveal many inconsistencies, and even whole words left blank to be filled in later. In addition to these difficulties with handwriting, spelling is inconsistent not only between individuals but even from one usage to the next within a document. While some of this variability may be attributed to attempts to record phonetic variation in pronunciation, much seems due to general laxity in spelling codes or even a fashion for individualized styles of writing.

These difficulties are compounded in the case of Smith by the fact that he was not an educated man, but a soldier. Even so, comparisons of Smith's vocabulary with other, better known Algonquian languages (e.g., Barbour 1971, 1972) suggest that he was surprisingly accurate; he even recorded the (often unstressed) initial vowels that are common in Powhatan, which were sometimes missed by others. He must be credited for having done an admirable job, under the circumstances, but his sometimes unwieldy vowel-strings and liberal use of end-of-syllable *gh* (the phonetic value of which is unclear) tell as much of his difficulties in trying to record the sounds he heard as they do of those sounds themselves.

There are several instances in this text in which the letter *v* appears as the first letter in a Powhatan word, or before a consonant. This represents one of the most common difficulties in works from this period, and results both from typographical usage and handwriting in which the two characters were used interchangeably. These appear-

3

ances of *v* should be read as *u*. In one word will be found the letter *ß*, which should be read as *ss*, as in modern German.

While there has been considerable scholarship on the Powhatan Indians in recent years (e.g., Rountree (1989, 1990), Feest (1990), and Gleach (1997)), there has been little new research on their language. This is partly due to changing academic interests, but largely because of an increased recognition of the limitations for linguistic analysis of such poorly recorded languages. At the turn of the century there were debates over classification and the meanings of individual words; there was a common feeling at the time that the reconstruction of meanings was possible if all available information could be brought together and subjected to the proper comparative analysis. The difficulties and dangers of such reconstruction became more clear as time passed, and today few are willing to even speculate on such matters when there is so much work to be done with languages that are still spoken, or at least are better recorded. Despite the limitations there are still possibilities for research on Powhatan, however, as Siebert's 1975 article demonstrated, and it is to be hoped that publication of this material will encourage such work.

Optimism concerning the reconstruction of meanings was tied to the ideas of salvage anthropology and linguistics early in this century; at least some Powhatan had still been spoken in the nineteenth century, and several small word-lists had been made in attempts to record what remained. The two word-lists of Pamunkey and Nansemond included in this volume are the best examples, and they

4

themselves are problematic. In both lists, the number one is the only word that can clearly be recognized as Powhatan (or even Algonquian), and most of the other words are completely unrecognizable. By the mid-nineteenth century Native people from several other nations, as well as non-Native people, had joined the Powhatan communities, and extensive language mixing –or even the creative genera-tion of new words –is possible; when Frank Speck worked with the Powhatans in the 1910's and 20's he noted that most of the words he collected appeared to be Ojibwe. Unfortunately, few outsiders in the eighteenth and nine-teenth centuries had any serious interest in the remnants of eastern nations like the Powhatans, and we will never be able to reconstruct much of what transpired over that time. Thomas Jefferson's assessment, in his *Notes on the State of Virginia*, that the Powhatan languages were dead was not correct at the time, but given the neglect and marginalization of the Powhatan people it proved pro-phetic. While the Powhatan people survive today, their original language can be studied only through documents such as the one presented here.

—Frederic W. Gleach 1997

References and Additional Readings

Barbour, Philip L. 1964. *The Three Worlds of Captain John Smith*. Boston: Houghton Mifflin.

Barbour, Philip L. 1971. "The Earliest Reconnaissance of the Chesapeake Bay Area: Captain John Smith's Map and Indian Vocabulary". *Virginia Magazine of History and Biography* 79(3):280-302.

Barbour, Philip L. 1972. "The Earliest Reconnaissance of the Chesapeake Bay Area: Captain John Smith's Map and Indian Vocabulary". Part II. *Virginia Magazine of History and Biography* 80(1):21-51.

Barbour, Philip L. (ed.). 1986. *The Complete Works of Captain John Smith (1580-1631) in Three Volumes*. Chapel Hill: University of North Carolina Press.

Bloomfield, Leonard. 1946. "Algonquian". In *Linguistic Structures of Native America*. Ed. Cornelius Osgood. Viking Fund Publications in Anthropology, no. 6. New York: Viking Fund.

Feest, Christian. 1990. *The Powhatan Tribes*. New York: Chelsea House.

Gerard, William R. 1904. "The Tapahanek dialect of Virginia". *American Anthropologist* n.s. 6(2):313-30.

Gleach, Frederic W. 1997. *Powhatan's World and Colonial Virginia: A Conflict of Cultures*. Lincoln: University of Nebraska Press.

Goddard, Ives. 1978a. "Eastern Algonquian Languages". In *Handbook of North American Indians*, vol. 15, *Northeast*. Ed. Bruce G. Trigger. Washington: Smithsonian Institution Press.

Goddard, Ives. 1978b. "Central Algonquian Languages". In *Handbook of North American Indians*, vol. 15, *Northeast*. Ed. Bruce G. Trigger. Washington: Smithsonian Institution Press.

Michelson, Truman. 1933. The Linguistic Classification of Powhatan. *American Anthropologist* 35(3):549.

Rountree, Helen C. 1989. *The Powhatan Indians of Virginia: Their Traditional Culture*. Norman: University of Oklahoma Press.

Rountree, Helen C. 1990. *Pocahontas's People: The Powhatan Indians of Virginia through Four Centuries*. Norman: University of Oklahoma Press.

Siebert, Frank T., Jr. 1975. "Resurrecting Virginia Algonquian from the Dead: The Reconstituted and Historical Phonology of Powhatan". In *Studies in Southeastern Indian Languages*. Ed. James M. Crawford. Athens: University of Georgia Press.

Excerpt from
The Voyages and Discoveries of Captain John Smith in Virginia

On the west side of the bay, we sayd were 5 faire and delightfull navigable rivers. The first of those, and the next to the mouth of the Bay hath his course from the West Northwest. It is called *Powhatan*, according to the name of a principall country that lyeth upon it. The mouth of this river is neare three myles in breadth, yet doe the shoules force the Channell so neare the land, that a Sacre will overshoot it at point blanke. It is navigable 150 myles, the shoules and soundings are here needlesse to be expressed. It falleth from Rockes farre west in a Country inhabited by a nation they call *Monacans*. But where it commeth into our discovery it is *Powhatan*. In the farthest place that was diligently observed, are falles, rockes, shoules, &c. which makes it past navigation any higher. Thence in the running downward, the river is enriched with many goodly brookes, which are maintained by an infinit number of small rundles and pleasant springs, that disperse themselves for best service, as do the veines of a mans body. From the South there fals into it: First, the pleasant river of *Apamatuck*. Next more to the East are two small rivers of *Quiyoughcohanocke*. A little farther is a Bay wherein falleth 3 or 4 prettie brookes & creekes that halfe intrench the Inhabitants of *Warraskoyac*, then the river of *Nandsamund*, and lastly the brooke of *Chisapeack*. From the North side is the river of *Chickahamania*, the backe river of *James*

Towne; another by the *Cedar Isle*, where we lived ten weekes upon Oysters, then a convenient harbour for Fisher boats at *Kecoughtan*, that so turneth it selfe into Bayes and Creekes, it makes that place very pleasant to inhabit; their cornefields being gided therein in a manner as Pensulaes. The most of these rivers are inhabited by severall nations, or rather families, of the name of the rivers. They have also over those some Governour, as their King, which they call *Werowances*. In a Peninsula on the North side of this river are the English Planted in a place by them called *James* Towne. in honour of the Kings most excellent Majestie.

The first and next the rivers mouth are the *Kecoughtans*, who besides their women & children, have not past 20 fighting men. The *Paspaheghes* (on whose land is seated *James* Towne, some 40 myles from the Bay) have not past 40. The river called *Chickahamania* neare 250. The *Weanocks* 100. The *Arrowhatocks* 30. The place called *Powhatan* some 40. On the South side this river the *Appamatucks* have sixtie fighting men. The *Qusyougcohancoks* 25. The *Nandsamunds* 200. The *Chesapeacks* 100. Of this last place the Bay beareth the name. In all these places is a severall commander, which they call *Werowance*, except the *Chickahamanians*, who are governed by the Priests and their Assistans, or their Elders called *Caw-cawwassoughes*. In sommer no place affordeth more plentie of Sturgeon, nor in winter more abundance of foule, especially in time of frost. I tooke once 52 Sturgeons at a draught, at another 68. From the later end of May till the end of June are taken few, but yong Sturgeons of two foot, or a yard long. From thence till the midst of September, them of two or three yards long and few others. And in 4 or 5, houres with one Net were ordinarily taken 7 or 8: often more, seldom lesse. In the small rivers all the yeare there is good plentie of small fish, so that with hookes those that would take paines had sufficient.

Foureteene myles Northward from the river *Powhatan*, is the river *Pamaunkee*, which is navigable 60 or 70 myles, but with Catches and small Barkes 30 or 40 myles farther. At the ordinary flowing of the salt water, it divideth it selfe into two gallant branches. On the South side inhabit the people of *Youghtanund*, who have about 60 men for warres. On the North branch *Mattapament*, who have 30 men. Where this river is divided the Country is called *Pamaunkee*, and nourisheth neare 300 able men. About 25 myles lower on the North side of this river is *Werawocomoco*, where their great King inhabited when I was delivered him prisoner; yet there are not past 40 able men. Ten or twelve myles lower, on the South side of this river, is *Chickiack*, which hath some 40 or 50 men. These, as also *Apamatuck*, *Irrohatock*, and *Powhatan*, are their great Kings chiefe alliance, and inhabitants. The rest his Conquests.

Before we come to the third river that falleth from the mountaines, there is another river (some 30 myles navigable) that commeth from the Inland, called *Payankatanke*, the Inhabitants are about 50 or 60 serviceable men.

The third navigable river is called *Toppahanock*. (This is navigable some 130 myles) At the top of it inhabit the people called *Mannahoacks* amongst the mountaines, but they are above the place we described. Upon this river on the North side are the people *Cuttatawomen*, with 30 fighting men. Higher are the *Moraughtacunds*, with 80. Beyond them *Rapahanock* with 100. Far above is another *Cuttatawomen* with 20. On the South is the pleasant seat of *Nantaughtacund* having 150 men. This river also as the two former, is replenished with fish and foule.

The fourth river is called *Patawomeke*, 6 or 7 myles in breadth. It is navigable 140 myles, and fed as the rest with many sweet rivers and springs, which fall from the bordering hils. These hils many of them are planted, and yeeld no lesse plentie and varietie of fruit, then the river exceedeth with abundance of fish. It is inhabited on both sides. First on the South side at the very entrance is *Wighcomoco* & hath some 130 men, beyond them *Sekacawone* with 30. The *Onawmanient* with 100. And the *Patawomekes* more than 200. Here doth the river divide it selfe into 3 or 4 convenient branches. The greatest of the least is called *Quiyough*, trending Northwest, but the river itselfe turneth Northeast, and is still a navigable streame. On the Westerne side of this bought is *Tauxenent* with 40 men. On the North of this river is *Secowocomoco* with 40. Somewhat further *Potapaco* with 20. In the East part is *Pamacaeack* with 60. After Moyowance with 100. And lastly, Nacotchtanke with 80. The river above this place maketh his passage downe a low pleasant valley overshaddowed in many places with high rocky mountaines; from whence distill innumerable sweet and pleasant springs.

The fift river is called *Pawtuxunt*, of a lesse proportion

then the rest; but the channell is 16 fadome deepe in some places. Here are infinit skuls of divers kindes of fish more then elswhere. Upon this river dwell the people called *Acquintanacksuak*, *Pawtuxunt*, and *Mattapanient*. Two hundred men was the greatest strength that could be there perceived. But they inhabit together, and not so dispersed as the rest. These of all other we found most civill to give intertainement.

Thirtie leagues Northward is a river not inhabited, yet navigable; for the red clay resembling *bole Armoniack* we called it *Bolus*. At the end of the Bay where it is 6 or 7 myles in breadth, it divides it selfe into 4 branches, the best commeth Northwest from among the mountaines, but though Canows may goe a dayes iourney or two up it, we could not get two myles up it with our boat for rockes. Upon it is seated the *Sasquesahanocks*, neare it North and by West runneth a creeke a myle and a halfe: at the head whereof the Eble left us on shore, where we found many trees cut with hatchets. The next tyde keeping the shore to seeke for some Salvages; (for within thirtie leagues fayling, we saw not any, being a barren Country,) we went up another small river like a creeke 6 or 7 myle. From thence returning we met 7 Canowes of the *Massowomeks*, with whom we had conference by signes, for we understood one another scarce a word: the next day we discovered the small river & people of *Tockwhogh* trending Eastward....

On the East side the *Bay*, is the river *Tockwhogh*, and upon it a people that can make 100 men, seated some seaven myles within the river: where they have a Fort very well pallisadoed and mantelled with barkes of trees. Next them is *Ozinies* with sixty men. More to the South of that East side of the *Bay*, the river *Rapahanock*, neere unto which is the river *Kuskarawaock*, Upon which is seated a people with 200 men. After that, is the river *Tants Wighcocomoco*, & on it a people with 100 men. The people of those rivers are of little stature, of another language from the rest, & very rude. But they on the river *Acohanock* with 40 men, & they of *Accomack* 80 men doth equalize any of the Territories of *Powhatan*, and speake his language, who over all those doth rule as King.

Southward we went to some parts of *Chawonock* and the *Mangoags* to search for them left by Mr. White. Amongst those people are thus many severall Nations of sundry Languages, that environ *Powhatans* Territories. The *Chawonockes*, the *Mangougs*, the *Monacans*, the *Mannahokes*, the *Masawomekes*, the *Powhatans*, the *Sasquesahanocks*, the *Atquanachukes*, the *Tockwoghes*, and the *Kuscarawaokes*. All those not any one understandeth another but by interpreters.

POWHATAN — ENGLISH

Accowprets, *shears.*

Aroughcun, *a beast much like a badger but used to live in trees as squirrels do.* (i.e. raccoon)

Assapanick, *flying squirrel.*

Assentamens, *peas.*

Attasskuss, *leaves, weeds, or grass.*

Attawp, *a bow.*

Attonce, *arrows.*

Aumouhhowgh, *a target.*

Case, *how many?*

Cattapeuk, *the Spring.*

Caucorouse, *captain.*

Caw-cawwassoughes, *governing elders.*

Chechinquamins, *a small fruit growing on little trees, husked like a chestnut, but the fruit most like a small acorn.* (i.e. chinquapin)

Chepsin, *land.*

Cohattayough, *the Summer.*

Comatinchtassapooeksku, *sixty.*

Comotinch, *six.*

Copotone, *sturgeon.*

Crenepo, *a woman.*

Kaskeke, *ten.*

Kekatawgh, *nine.*

Kekataughtassapooeksku, *ninety.*

Kekughes, *lives.*

Keskowghes, *suns.*

Macocks, *a fruit like a muskmelon.*

Maracocks, *a wild fruit much like a lemon.*

Marowanchesso, *a boy.*

Marrapough, *enemies.*

Maskapow, *the worst of enemies.*

Matchcores, *skins* or *garments.*

Mattaßin, *copper.*

Mattoum, *groweth as our Bents. The seed is not much unlike to Rye though much smaller. This they use for a dainty bread buttered with deer suet.*

Mawchick chammay, *the best of friends.*

Messamins, *a sort of grape nearly as high as a cherry.*

Mockasins, *shoes.*

Monacookes, *swords.*

Musquaspen, *a root the bigness of a finger, and as red as blood. This they use to paint their mats, targets, and such like.*

Mussascus, *a beast of the form and nature of our water rats, but many of them smell exceedingly strongly of musk.* (i.e. muskrat)

Musses, *woods.*

Necut, *one.*

Necuttoughtysinough, *one hundred.*

Necuttwevnquaough, *one thousand.*

Nemarough, *a man.*

18

Nepawweshowghs, *moons.*

Nepinough, *the season for the earing of their corn.*

Netoppew, *friends.*

Ningh, *two.*

Ninghsapooeksku, *twenty.*

Noughmass, *fish.*

Nuss, *three.*

Nussapooeksku, *thirty.*

Nussswashtassapooeksku, *eighty.*

Nusswash, *eight.*

Ocoughtanamnis, *a berry much like capers which grows in the watery valleys.*

Okees, *Gods.*

Opassom, *a beast with the head of a swine, a tail like a rat, and the bigness of a cat. Under her belly she has a bag where she lodges, carries, and suckles her young.* (i.e. opossum)

Osies, *heavens.*

Pamesacks, *knives.*

Parankestassapooeksku, *fifty.*

Paranske, *five.*

Pausarowmena, *a rare dish, made of corn boiled with beans.*

Pawcohiccora, *walnut milk.*

Pawcorances, *altar stones.*

Pawcussacks, *guns.*

Pawpaxsoughes, *years.*

Pawpecones, *pipes.*

Pemmenaw, *a kind of grass used to make thread.*

Pocones, *a small root that grows in the mountains, which being dried and beat in powder turns red. And this they use for swellings, aches, anointing their joints, painting their heads and garments.*

Pokatawer, *fire.*

Ponap, *bread.*

Popanow, *the Winter.*

Pummahumps, *stars.*

Pungnough, *an ear of corn burned to powder, for mingling with meals.*

Putchamins, *a plum which grows as high as a* Palmeta: *the fruit is like a Medler; it is first green, then yellow, and red when it is ripe.*

Quiyoughcosoughs, *petty Gods, and their affinities.*

Rawcomens, *a berry much like our gooseberry.*

Rawcosowghs, *days.*

Righcomoughes, *deaths.*

Sawwehone, *blood.*

Shacquohocan, *a stone.*

Suckahanna, *water.*

Taquitock, *the harvest season and fall of leaves.*

Tockahacks, *pickaxes.*

Tockawhoughe, *the chief root they have for food.*

Tomahacks, *axes.*

Toppawoss, *seven.*

Toppawousstassapooeksku, *seventy.*

Toppquough, *nights.*

Tussan, *beds.*

Ussawassin, *iron, brass, silver, or any white metal.*

Ustatahamen, *a food made of bran boiled with water.*

Utchunquoyes, *wild cat.*

Weghshaughes, *flesh.*

Wepenter, *a cuckold.*

Werowance, *king, commander.*

Wighsacan, *a small root which cures their hurts and diseases.*

Yehawkans, *houses.*

Yowgh, *four.*

Yowghapooeksku, *forty.*

Phrases

Ka ka torawincs yowo? *What do you call this?*

Casacunnakack, peya quagh acquintan vttasantasough. *In how many days will there come here any more English ships?*

Mowchick woyawgh tawgh noeragh kaquere mecher. *I am very hungry, what shall I eat?*

Tawnor nehiegh Powhatan. *Where dwells Powhatan?*

Mache, nehiegh yourowgh, Orapaks. *Now he dwells a great way hence at Orapaks.*

Vittapitchewayne anpechitchs nehawper Werowacomoco. *You lie, he stayed over at Werowacomoco.*

Kator nehiegh mattagh neer vttapitchewayne. *Truly he is there, I do not lie.*

Spaughtynere keragh werowance mawmarinough kekaten wawgh peyaquaugh. *Run you then to the King Mawmarynough and bid him come hither.*

Vtteke, e peya weyack wighwhip. *Get you gone, and come again quickly.*

Kekaten Pokahontas patiaquagh niugh tanks manotyens neer mowchick rawrenock audowgh. *Bid Pocahontas bring two little baskets here, and I will give her white beads to make her a chain.*

ENGLISH — POWHATAN

Altar stones, *pawcorances*.

Arrows, *attonce*.

Axes, *tomahacks*.

Beds, *tussan*.

Berry, like capers, *ocoughtanamnis*. **Like a gooseberry**, *rawcomens*.

Blood, *sawwehone*.

Bow, a, *attawp*.

Boy, *marowanchesso*.

Brass, *ussawassin*.

Bread, *ponap*.

Captain, *caucorouse*.

Cat, wild, *utchunquoyes*.

Chinquapin, *chechinquamins*.

Commander, *werowance*.

Copper, *mattaβin*.

Corn, an ear of burned to powder, *pungnough*.

Cuckold, *wepenter*.

Days, *rawcosowghs*.

Deaths, *righcomoughes*.

Eight, *nusswash*.

Eighty, *nussswashtassapooeksku*.

Elders, governing, *caw-cawwassoughes*.

Enemies, *marrapough*. **The worst of enemies**, *maskapow*.

Fifty, *parankestassapooeksk.*

Fire, *pokatawer.*

Fish, *noughmass.*

Five, *paranske.*

Flesh, *weghshaughes.*

Food, made of corn and beans, *pausarowmena.* **Food made of bran and boiled water**, *ustatahamen.*

Forty, *yowghapooeksku.*

Four, *yowgh.*

Friends, *netoppew.* **The best of friends**, *mawchick chammay.*

Fruit, like a small acorn, *chechinquamins.* **Like a muskmelon**, *macocks.* **Like a lemon**, *maracocks.* **Like a sort of grape**, *messamins.* **A berry like capers**, *ocoughtanamnis.* **Like a plum or medler**, *putchamins.* **A berry like a gooseberry**, *rawcomens.*

Garments, *matchcores.*

Gods, *okees.* **Petty gods and their affinities**, *quiyoughcosoughs.*

Grass, *attasskuss.* **A kind of grass used to make thread**, *pemmenaw.* **A type of grass like bents**, *mattoum.*

Guns, *pawcussacks.*

Heavens, *osies.*

Houses, *yehawkans.*

How many?, *case.*

Iron, *ussawassin.*

King, *werowance.*
Knives, *pamesacks.*

Land, *chepsin.*
Leaves, *attasskuss.*
Lives, *kekughes.*

Man, *nemarough.*
Metal, any white, *ussawassin.*
Milk, walnut, *pawcohiccora.*
Moons, *nepawweshowghs.*
Muskrat, *mussascus.*

Nights, *toppquough.*
Nine, *kekatawgh.*
Ninety, *kekataughtassapooeksku.*

One, *necut.*
One hundred, *necuttoughtysinough.*
One thousand, *necuttwevnquaough.*
Opossum, *opassom.*

Peas, *assentamens.*
Pickaxes, *tockahacks.*
Pipes, *pawpecones.*

Raccoon, *aroughcun.*

Root, red used for painting, *musquaspen.* **Mountain root used for swellings, aches, and painting**, *pocones.* **Their chief root for food**, *tockawhoughe.* **Small root which cures their hurts and diseases**, *wighsacan.*

Season, for earing corn, *nepinough.* **Harvest season**, *taquitock*

Seven, *toppawoss.*

Seventy, *toppawousstassapooeksku.*

Shears, *accowprets.*

Shoes, *mockasins.*

Silver, *ussawassin.*

Six, *comotinch.*

Sixty, *comatinchtassapooeksku.*

Skins, *matchcores.*

Spring, the, *cattapeuk.*

Squirrel, flying, *assapanick.*

Stars, *pummahumps.*

Stone, a, *shacquohocan.*

Sturgeon, *copotone.*

Summer, the, *cohattayough.*

Suns, *keskowghes.*

Swords, *monacookes.*

Target, a, *aumouhhowgh.*

Ten, *kaskeke.*

Thirty, *nussapooeksku.*

Three, *nuss.*
Twenty, *ninghsapooeksku.*
Two, *ningh.*

Walnut milk, *pawcohiccora.*
Water, *suckahanna.*
Weeds, *attasskuss.*
Wild cat, *utchunquoyes.*
Winter, the, *popanow.*
Woman, *crenepo.*
Woods, *musses.*

Years, *pawpaxsoughes.*

Numerical Table

1. Necut
2. Ningh
3. Nuss
4. Yowgh
5. Paranske
6. Comotinch
7. Toppawoss
8. Nusswash
9. Kekatawgh
10. Kaskeke

20. Ninghsapooeksku
30. Nussapooeksku
40. Yowghapooeksku
50. Parankestassapooeksku
60. Comatinchtassapooeksku
70. Toppawousstassapooeksku
80. Nussswashtassapooeksku
90. Kekataughtassapooeksku
100. Necuttoughtysinough
1000. Necuttweunquaough

PAMUNKEY
WORD-LIST

The following words were found still surviving in 1844, at the Indian Pamunkey town, in King William County, Va. They were collected by Rev. Mr. Dalrymple, who gave me a copy of them. C.C.

Petersburg, Va., April 23d, 1858.

Tonshee, *son*.
Nucksee, *daughter*.
Petucka, *cat*.
Kayyo, *thankfulness*.
O-ma-yah, *O my Lord*.
Kenaanee, *friendship*.
Baskonee, *thank you*.
Eeskut, *go out dog*.
Nikkut, *one*.
Orijak, *two*.
Kiketock, *three*.
Mitture, *four*.
Nahnkitty, *five*.
Vomtally, *six*.
Talliko, *seven*.
Tingdum, *eight*.
Yantay, *ten*.

NANSEMOND
WORD-LIST

They [the Nansemond] have entirely lost their aboriginal language and customs, if we except their devotion to the water, and differ but little from their white neighbors. According to the statements of several persons of middle age, their parents some fifty years ago had conversational knowledge of the old language. Even this knowledge must have been limited, as the present writer, by the most careful search, could find but one old man, William W. Weaver, a Nansemond, from whom even half a dozen words could be obtained. He was then so feeble, mentally and physically, that he could not be questioned with any satisfation. He died about a year later, in 1902, and with him faded away the last echo of Powhatan as a living language. From the distribution of the original tribes and former jealousies, it is probable that the language had several well-marked dialects.

On account of the old man's condition, even the half-dozen words obtained from him needed confirmation by his son, then fifty-three years of age, who claimed to have remembered them from his father.

—James Mooney, 1907

Nĭkătwĭn, *one.*
Näkătwĭn, *two.*
Nikwásăti, *three.*
Toisíaw', *four.*
Mishä´ naw, *five.*
Marímo, *dog.*

Also available in the American Language Reprint Series

For more information on the series, see our website at:
www.evolpub.com/ALR/ALRbooks.html